THE OXFORD PIANO METHOD

P·I·A·N·O T·I·M·E
S·I·G·H·T-R·E·A·D·I·N·G

B·O·O·K
2

Pauline Hall and Fiona Macardle

MUSIC DEPARTMENT

OXFORD
UNIVERSITY PRESS

OXFORD
UNIVERSITY PRESS

Great Clarendon Street, Oxford OX2 6DP
198 Madison Avenue, New York, NY10016, USA

Oxford University Press is a department of the University of Oxford
and furthers the University's aim of excellence in research, scholarship,
and education by publishing worldwide in

Oxford New York
Athens Auckland Bangkok Bogotá Buenos Aires Calcutta
Cape Town Chennai Dar es Salaam Delhi Florence Hong Kong Istanbul
Karachi Kuala Lumpur Madrid Melbourne Mexico City Mumbai
Nairobi Paris São Paulo Singapore Taipei Tokyo Toronto Warsaw

and associated companies in Berlin Ibadan

Oxford is a registered trademark of Oxford University Press

3 5 7 9 10 8 6 4

ISBN 0-19-372769-2

Music originated by Seton Music Graphics Ltd., Ireland

Book design by Barbara Prentiss

Printed in Great Britain on acid-free paper by
Halstan & Co. Ltd., Amersham, Bucks.

INTRODUCTION

Every time you play a new piece of music, it's like going on an adventure into unknown territory. You should plan ahead and look around carefully to see what obstacles and dangers are lying in wait.

In Book 1 you got used to checking the little code-signs at the beginning of each piece. These reminded you to check for the many dangers that might be lurking. In this book, you'll find the main code-signs are at the beginning of each new stage, but there will still be code-signs at the beginning of some pieces where there are special hazards.

Never embark on a piece of sight-reading without first checking for each of these:

 Look at the key. Are there any sharps or flats?

 Look at the time signature. It's sensible to count out loud (even if it's in a whisper) all the way.

 Look out for tied notes.

 Danger point—look out!

 Look out for tricky rhythms.

 Skips and jumps (miss a note or two).

 Expression—makes your playing much more interesting and musical.

 Watch out for fingering.

Golden Rules of Sight-reading

1. Always count! A steady beat is very important.

2. Good explorers never stop or look back.

Dangers ahead!

REMEMBER: never embark on a sight-reading journey without first checking your code-signs.

2 The code-sign for a rest is ![rest] There are lots in the next piece!

3 👓 You must count like mad in this piece! Don't get caught out!

4 Add the code-signs which you think would help someone else to play the next piece. Draw them in the box.

4

L·O·O·K A·N·D G·U·E·S·S

When you're sight-reading, it helps if you can look at music and guess what it sounds like. Here are some guessing games. Play middle C before each one to help you.

Look at this box. What does it sound like? Don't play it yet—just think it to yourself and imagine you're playing it.

Now sing it, and play it to check. Were you right?

Look at the next box. (Play middle C first.)

Think . . . sing . . . check.
Were you right? Go on to the next box.

LK out! This one's more difficult.
Think . . . sing . . . check.

Now some more. Choose any box you like. Play middle C before you guess each one.

Try these again sometime. You'll get better at guessing.

STAGE 2

Oops! Watch out!

ACCIDENTALS are easy because they give themselves away!
Watch carefully and don't have any accidents with them!
They only last for the bar in which they appear.

◄ ◄ Are you still checking for these?

This code sign tells you there are some tricky notes—accidentals—ahead.
Look first, then plan your route before you begin, so you don't trip!

Are these still flat? Why?

Take your time with this one! This is a **natural** sign. It cancels out any sharp or flat before it.

Marcato

Is this still a sharp?

6

Why is this one a natural?

S·T·A·G·E 3

Up, up and away!

LEGER LINES sound as if they might give you wrinkles. 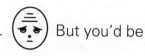 But you'd be worrying over nothing!

These mysterious invisible lines are always there but only appear when they are needed, just like the genie in Aladdin. They climb the same ladder as all the other notes. For the moment you only need three of them, all for your left hand.

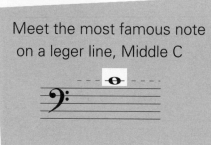

Meet the most famous note on a leger line, Middle C

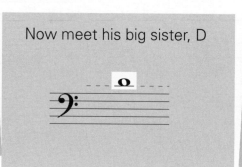

Now meet his big sister, D

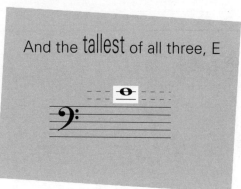

And the **tallest** of all three, E

 This code-sign, a ladder, reminds you to check for leger lines.

Allegretto

8

2 **Brightly**

3 **Steadily**

4 **Rhythmic**

5 **Flowing**

C·O·M·I·N·G TO THE R·E·S·C·U·E

The composer of the next piece of music must have been in a hurry! Lots of things have been missed out.

You are an editor. Go through the piece carefully putting in things which are needed, and any 'extras' like expression marks which might improve it. Fingering would also help.

Your turn to be the composer now. Can you write a piece for your friends to sight-read? To make it fairly easy for them, it should:

♦ only use the notes C D E F G.
♦ the left hand should play the first two bars.
♦ the right hand should play the last two bars.

The notes shouldn't jump around too much.

A rhythm pattern has been added but you don't have to use it—make up your own if you like.

Which code-signs would be helpful at the beginning? Write them in.

End on C.

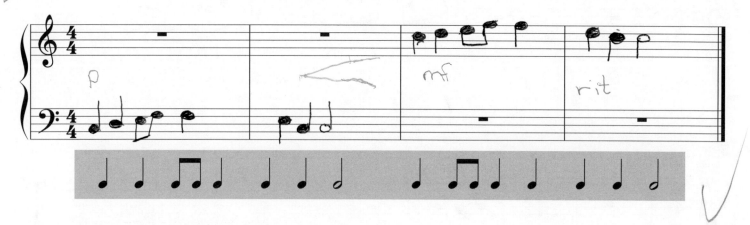

Here are some expression marks you could use:

p   *mf*   *rit.*

Hop, skip, and jump

One of the secrets of being able to find your way in a dense musical jungle is being able to spot how far away notes are from each other.

For instance, you can see straight away that these two notes 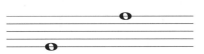 are far apart

and these two  are very close together.

You are used to skips, which go from a space to the next space

or a line to the next line. These are called **thirds**.

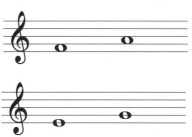

Now for some jumps.

Fourths jump over two white keys. They look like this:

They *look* wider than thirds, don't they?

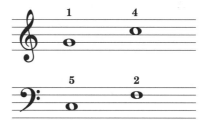

Fifths jump over three white keys. They're easy to spot!

They go from a space to the next space but one,

or a line to the next line but one.

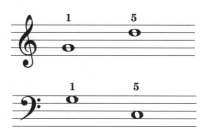

Try playing some thirds, fourths, and fifths so that you get used to the feel of them.

LO👀K out! There's loads of 🏃 everywhere!

Quick as you can! Play these and say whether they're thirds, fourths, or fifths:

Play a third   Play a fifth

(Write them here.)

12

STAGE 5

Obstacles ahead

Now you have to navigate a tricky part of your journey! You're ready to have a go at putting your hands together—but don't panic, because one hand will be doing most of the work for quite a long time to come!

Remember to check **everything** before you set off:

The key signature?

Any difficult fingering?

The time signature?

Any tricky skips or jumps?

Any rhythmic difficulties?

Any notes on leger lines?

Any hazardous places?

Any rests?   Or ties?

Any accidentals?

Any expression marks?

What code-signs would you add to the next piece? Draw the ones you think would help in the box.

Now play it!

2

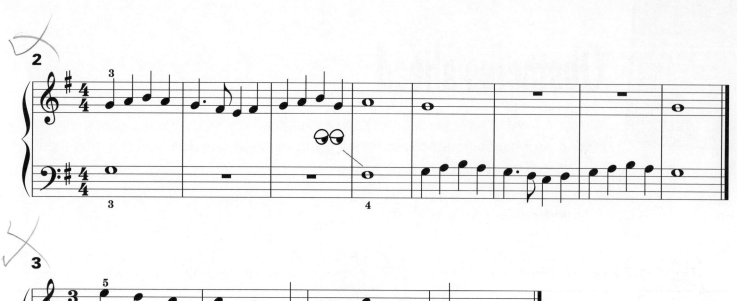

3

Don't get the idea that because you can't hear them, rests aren't important—just the opposite!

4

LOOK
ahead

Do you recognize this tune?

5 You need to look well ahead here. Your hands are really jumping about!

Steady does it

In this stage your left hand has a little more exploring to do than before. Try not to have a gap at the barline when you have to work out new notes in *both* hands.

Don't forget. Check for all of these *before* you begin.

1

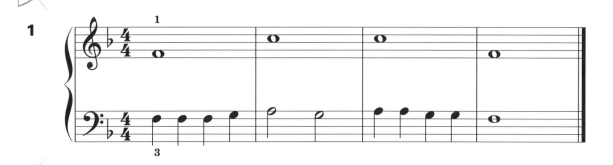

2 Check the left hand. What is the sharp?

3 Don't move your hand once you have placed it!

4

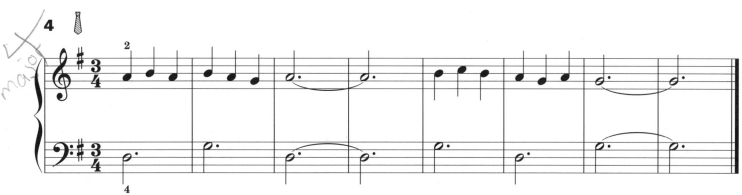

Always L👀K ahead as you play.

5 How many different notes does your right hand play?

6 Check your left hand notes before you set off.

Lots of people race ahead, only to stop dead at each barline to consider what to do next. But a bar line is like a hurdle—you must jump straight over, and keep going to the end. The best hurdlers do all their considering before they start! Find all the obstacles first, place your hands, then play.

Remember the tortoise—slow but sure!

FINISH

What about that **dotted rhythm?** Are you looking out for it?

Clap this rhythm:

One   two - oo three four

Now tie the first two notes:

This looks different but sounds the same:

Clap this first, and then play it:

16

Now one for your left hand.  (F♯s)

Here are a few more tunes to try:

 (B♭s)

LOOK carefully at the next piece, but don't play it until you've answered the clue-questions.
(The bars are numbered to make it easier.)

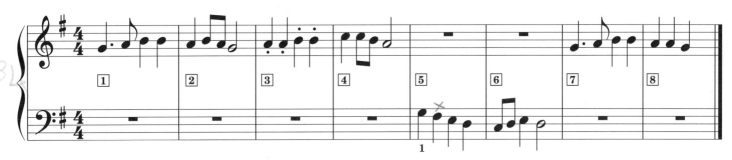

What key is it in? | G major

F sharp is played once—in which bar? | 5 | Mark it with an X.

Two bars are exactly the same. They are bar | 1 | and bar | 7

Can you spot a mistake? It's in bar | 8

In which bar are the notes played staccato? | 3

NOW PLAY IT!

S·T·A·G·E 7

Striding out

Up to now, when your hands have played together, one has only had long notes while the other is busy. Now it's time for both hands to be a little more equal. For the moment only one hand will move at a time. Many of the tunes in these exercises chase one another from hand to hand—can you spot which ones?

1

2

3 👓 F♯s in left hand.

4 👓 B♭s in both hands.

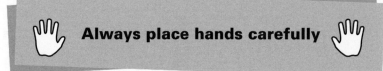

🖐 **Always place hands carefully** 🖐

5 👓👓 Keep your right hand hovering here, ready to play.

6 👓👓 Which hand is the busy one in this piece?

Watch your left hand. LOOK ahead ➡

7 **Restfully**

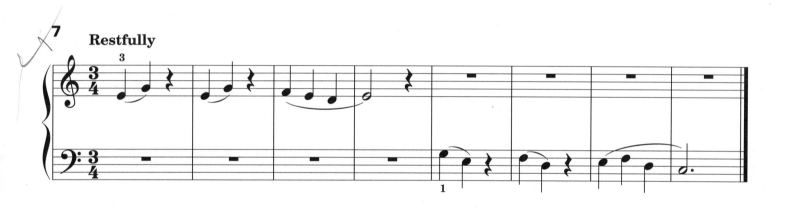

8

B·E·A·T THE B·A·N·D·I·T·S

A dangerous music gang has been at work!
But you—the great detective—can outwit them.

They have altered the next piece.
Draw a ring round anything that is wrong.

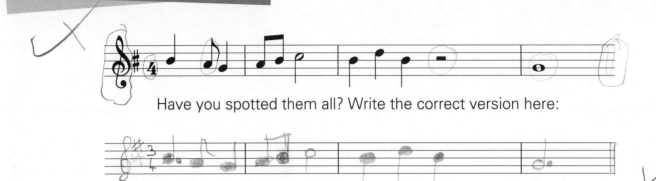

Have you spotted them all? Write the correct version here:

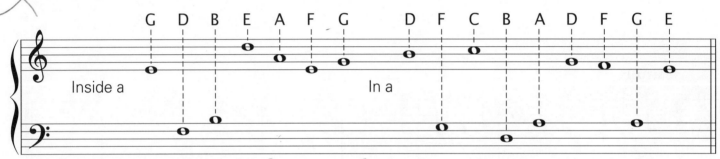

The gang has labelled the notes below to throw you off the trail. But if you cross out the *wrong* letter names and draw a ring round the *right* ones they should give you the name of the place where the next clues are hidden.

You found them inside a _B_ _A_ _G_ in a _C_ _A_ _F_ _E_ .

Now you can relax in the

C A F E

and have an

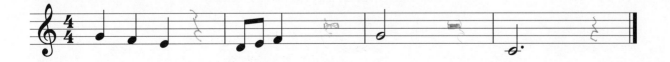

I C E C R E A M

All the rests in the piece of music below have been stolen by the gang. But you have found them! Put them back in their right places. To give you a clue here are three rests you might use.

20

5 This is a tricky piece! Your hands echo each other—but not quite.

6

Tick these check point boxes to help you remember.

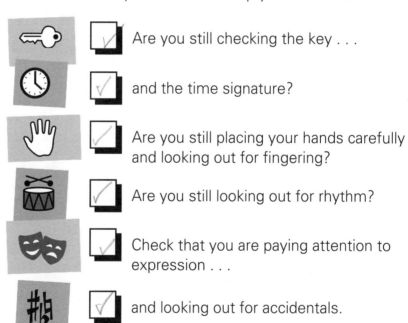

Are you still checking the key . . .

and the time signature?

Are you still placing your hands carefully and looking out for fingering?

Are you still looking out for rhythm?

Check that you are paying attention to expression . . .

and looking out for accidentals.

Are you ready for any notes on leger lines . . .

or any tricky skips or jumps?

Once you've started, check you aren't stopping.

Check that you're still counting all the way through—every bar!

Meet the challenge

The next pieces are a bit more challenging than the previous ones encountered on your journey. A little more preparation is needed, so check everything well before you set off. Keep calm and keep going!

1

2

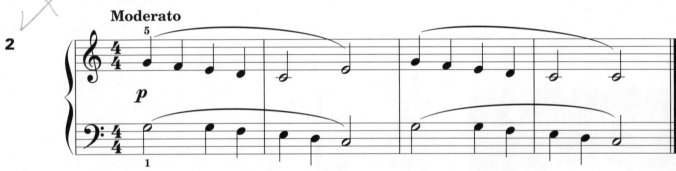

3 B♭s in right hand.

More About Accidentals

Although sharps and flats are *called* accidentals, they're not there by accident: they're there for a purpose. They aren't included in the key signature, but are added to the music as it goes along. Look out for them—they are important and if you neglect them things will go very wrong!

Don't forget—a **natural sign** ♮ cancels any sharp or flat which has gone before it. Try this little tune for your left hand.

Draw a ring around any sharps or naturals.

22

The first two of these pieces are played with separate hands. This should help you to be extra careful of the accidentals.

4 Lento

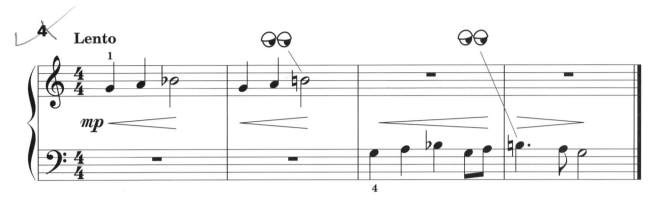

5 Expression marks are important too!

Brightly

6 Maestoso

7 Beware of the rest.

8 Leger lines in sight!

Rocking

9 🎭 Get ready!

Doloroso

Do you recognize this tune?

10

11 🎭

12 Legato

13 🔑 🕐 🥁 🎭 👓 Rather a lot to look out for here!

REMEMBER, when you come across any expression marks or signs you don't know, look them up and write them in your music note-book.

24

J·I·G·S·A·W T·U·N·E

On each jigsaw piece is a bar of a tune. They're all in the treble clef.
When you have decided how they fit, write their numbers in the boxes
below each one. Then copy out the four bars to make a tune.

Now play the whole thing!

Super Sight-Reader's

C·R·A·F·T·Y
Q·U·I·Z!

Don't try playing the piece below until you've checked all the clue-questions. Score 5 points for each clue you get right and add up your points at the end.

Score

1   When you're sight-reading, is it better to:

a) ~~keep looking back in case you've made a mistake?~~   **or**   b) look ahead so that you can see what's coming?

(Cross out the wrong answer.)

| 5 |

2   This rhythm ♩. ♪ is worth how many crotchets?   2

| 5 |

3   One of these sharps is meant to be an F sharp. Which one?
(Circle the right one.)

| 5 |

4   Would you play gradually louder or softer when you see this sign?   ◁   Louder

| 5 |

5   The key signature of the music below tells you to look out for a black key. Which one?   B♭

| 5 |

6   There are two bars where you'll have to be especially careful about the rhythm. They are bars __3__ and __5__ .

| 5 |

7   What accidental will you play?   C♯

| 5 |

8   How many bars have leger line notes in them (including middle C)?   3

| 5 |

Now play it and score an extra 25 points if you get it right!

| 22 |

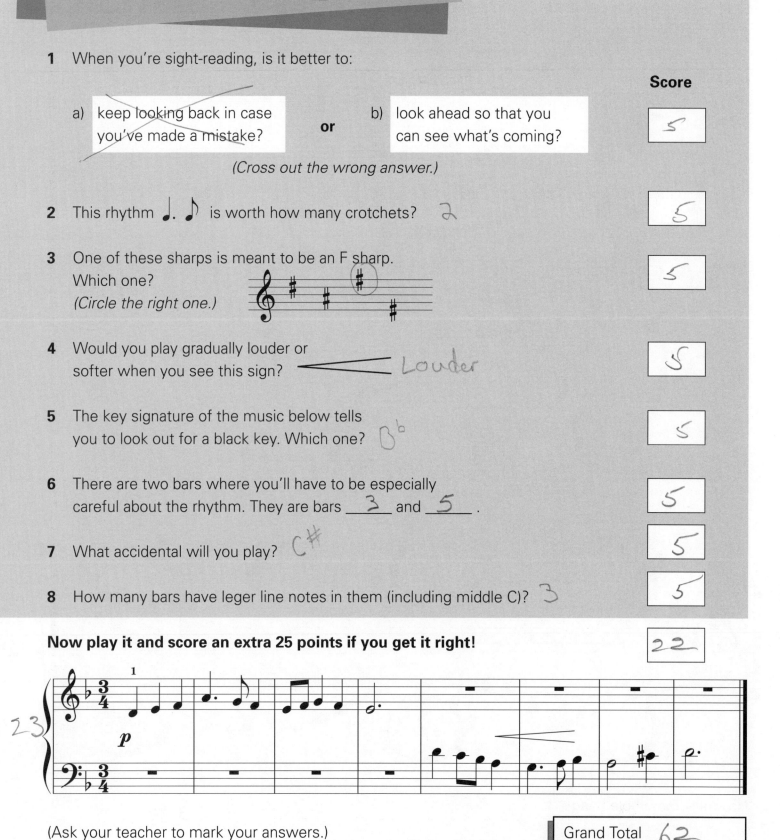

p

1 2 3

(Ask your teacher to mark your answers.)

Grand Total 62

Good.

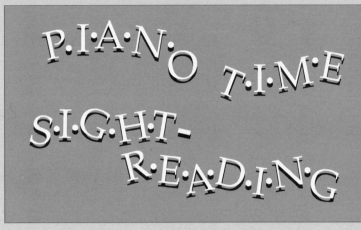

P·I·A·N·O T·I·M·E S·I·G·H·T- R·E·A·D·I·N·G

CERTIFICATE

This is to certify that

_____

is a
SUPER SIGHT- READER

and has completed

PIANO TIME SIGHT-READING
BOOK 2

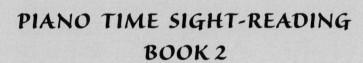

TEACHER'S SIGNATURE   DATE